CW00433285

LIFEL]

Volume 3

in an
occasional series
of often 'Occasional' poems

Proceeds to Prostate Cancer UK

Book Information

Copyright © Phil Poyser 2022
All rights reserved

The right of Phil Poyser as the author of this work has
been asserted by him in accordance with the Berne
Convention.

First published in Great Britain in 2022 by Poetry Doctor
Publications.

ISBN 978-1-7391915-0-4

All rights reserved. No part of this publication may be
reproduced, stored in a retrieval system, or transmitted,
in any form or by any means, electronic, mechanical,
photocopying, recording, or otherwise, without the prior
permission of the publisher or copyright owner.

Cover illustration copyright © Charlie Heathcote 2020.

In 'Lifelines', Phil Poyser has brought together a kaleidoscope of subjects, ranging from speculations on the origins of the universe to a rap concerning social justice; from a beech tree-shaped poem to a self-assembly poem kit from IKEA; from an 8 poem series based on images seared in an instant onto the retina to 4 well-known poems and a song parodied with intent.

Seven poems in the collection were inspired by the goings on at Brookfield Lane Allotment Association. (And if you like these, you might be interested in Phil's fourth volume, BLAA BLAA, Black Sheep, which focuses on allotment life and contains these poems and many more.)

As with Phil's previous poetry books, proceeds from sales of this collection are donated:

Proceeds to Prostate Cancer UK.

Contents

Image-spiration for 'Mount Rushmore' ~ p. 110

Lifelines: Crossing Words with Death

Dedicated to the memory of
John Anthony 'Tony' Platt ('Platty')
24th September, 1944 to 24th February, 2017

I stand at the back of the chapel,
peering over the heads of those filling the pews,
your soberly clad family and friends,
neighbours and workmates.
I'm fascinated by the splendid, eco-friendly isolation
of your lily-laden, wicker coffin.

Here I am saying my goodbyes,
39 years to the day, since my Dad's departure.
Thoughts turn past images of picnic hampers,
past laundry days to those distant, steam-powered
journeys his pigeons made in their baskets,
cooing their fear from crops, rhythmically nodding
from dowling-barred apertures.
How apt it would have been to send Dad off
on his final chuck in one made to measure.

In the cellar, one of his pigeon baskets waits, ready.

Back Track

We were so excited, we didn't sleep
a wink. Would morning never come and creep
through curtains' dangling veil, so we could leap
from out constricting sheets and rush downstairs,
pulling on a rumpled shirt and odd sock pairs?
Would rain come spoil it all? Or shine? Our prayers
were answered: a timid sun; a patch of blue
and Mam organised, unfussed, cried, 'Use the loo.'
Time's hurtling by and I can only find one shoe.
At last we're ready, frothy little imps,
and stare from platform's edge to catch first glimpse
of steam train's chuff to head for sand and shrimps.

From present day perspective, strange to confess,
our day trip out to almost-seaside town, Skegness,
held for us the magic of the Orient Express.

Anno Domini: A Walk Down Memory Lane

Dedicated to the memory of Philip Turner, who died aged 68 on 22nd August, 2016

We used to bounce along these woodland routes,
an hour snatched in lunchtime pause,
for keeping fit or just because
the springtime sun was shining. Now in boots

and double-wrapped, near bubble-wrapped, we tramp,
a modest, gentle, walking pace,
consistent with our ageing grace,
and Goretex®-clad, thus keeping out the damp.

Where once quick shower was grabbed
      before next meeting
with spirits high and cheeks bright flushed,
we change our boots and won't be rushed,
lick our lips as thoughts now turn to eating.

We'll sip a beer and ponder on fled youth.
We've walked a way down memory lane,
seen flashbacks of young selves again
and reconcile our present selves to truth.

Childhood Photograph

The photo is in black and white.
It dates from the early fifties.
This might be its diamond jubilee year.
It shows a young boy
on the front lawn of a semi.
He peers, squinting into the sun
and the camera lens.
And behind the camera?
His Mam? A friend? Not his Dad.
His Dad won't be home from the pit yet.
By the boy's feet, a dog relaxes,
tongue lolling in the heat.
The dog, a smooth-haired fox terrier,
is lean, alert, intelligent.
It's the boy who is chubby with puppy fat.
He will cry for a week when his dog is run over.
He will cry less when his Dad dies
or even ten years after that, for his Mam.
He does not know that very soon
he will be me.

D-V-1-0-R-C-E

With nods to Dolly Parton and Tammy Wynette's hit,
"D-I-V-O-R-C-E"

D-V-1-0-R-C-E[*], my new car's number plate.
I chose the latest model when the judge ruled –
      'Separate.'
You'd played the field and been a **H-double-E-L** to me,
so, my **L-O-T-U-S** plates spell '**D-V-1-0-R-C-E.**'

Sunroof rolled back, away I **S-P-double-E-D**.
I shoot off fast as you're now **P-A-S-T** to me.
The **A-L-I-M-O-N-Y** is a challenge with one end.
I'm **D-V-1-0-R-C-E-D** and learning how to spend.
I'm **D-V-1-0-R-C-E-D** and learning how to spend.

*Number plate seen in south Manchester in February 2015

Beech

This morning
it towered 50 feet above the *Leylandii* fronds.
Last year,
rooks had nested in its canopy and swayed precariously
- like today -
as if full sail on choppy seas, running before a
sou'wester.
On such a day,
surely the only danger is ceding to the gusting gale,
tearing and tugging at those roots.
Ah, not so,
for swarming up like a rigging monkey,
roped and helmeted, with chain-saw dangling,
comes the arboreal nemesis of standing proud.
Abseiling
from one pitch to another, he picks off
branch after branch, each carefully lowered or crashing down
according to its girth, then metre lengths of trunk
and skull-busting slices, thudding to earth,
till just the
bare stump
remains, stark
reminder of
centenarian's
former glory.

Blind Justice

Now listen to me, people, come and listen to my rap.
Take that i-phone from your ear
        and that i-pad off your lap.
We may think that there is justice,
        that Britain's fair and square,
but whilst we're feeling warm and snug,
        I'm goin' to stop you there,
'cos if you're black or Asian or live in a cardboard box,
lie in blankets in shop doorways,
        it's the school of hard knocks.
Yeah, it's the school of hard knocks
        and so on your house a pox
Yeah, so on your house a pox.

They've got her on Old Bailey's roof,
        weighing scales in her hand.
She holds a sword, a blindfold wears, impartial.
        Ain't she grand?
But she needs to shed those scales
        from her hand and from her eyes,
'cos the papers badmouth the poor
        and fill our heads with lies:

'They're scroungers on benefits.
          They don't want to earn their keep.
They spurn zero hours contracts.
          They'd rather booze and sleep.
Yeah, they'd rather booze and sleep,
          those expletives, bleep, bleep, bleep
Yeah, expletives, bleep, bleep, bleep.

They come from Eastern Europe,
          the Slav, the Lat, the Pole
and queue with home-grown parasites
          to claim the bloody dole.
Whilst, decent folk, that's you and me,
          work our effin' socks off,
they live the life of Riley, get stoned
          and get their rocks off.
They're busy havin' one more kid to get <u>*our*</u> *council flats*
and we know that generation will be dirty, little brats.

Yeah, they'll be dirty little brats.
It's backed up by the stats.
Yeah, it's backed up by the stats.'

So, while Murdoch and the Tory press,
   master puppeteers,
vomit out their headlines and so
   manipulate our fears,
Blind Justice stands there rigid
   with her back to City's banks,
turns deaf ear to austerity
   when the boardroom's saying 'Thanks'
with bonuses exceeding those
   of football transfer fees.

But I think I saw Blind Justice cry
   and get down on her knees.
Yeah, she got down on her knees
   to clean up all the sleaze.
Yeah, at last clean up the sleaze.

Drabble: The Spider in the Bath

*A Drabble is a poem or story told in exactly 100 words
(excluding the title).*

What does it live on, the spider in the bath?
It's not a great place for flies to cross its path,
yet it's fit and healthy and obviously clean,
roams end to end its vast domain from what I've seen.
There's no sign of woven web between the taps.
Is it that it hasn't spinnerets perhaps?
Every ploy it uses of arachnid guile
to coax all its nutrients out of bathroom tile,
but when it's time for me to soak away the gunge,
Incey Wincey's there, so I can't take the plunge,
Unless… I might just de-spider with the sponge!

Flood

Written at Lulworth Cove Holiday Fellowship after
Graham S. inadvertently flooded his bathroom

Water, water, everywhere, and all the boards did shrink.
Water, water, everywhere. To Graham, what's the link?

Here we are in Lulworth Cove,
     which nestles down in Dorset.
Day two and there's a panic.
     Can you guess the source? It's
when Colin spied some water
     flowing beneath the door,
watched horrified as inexorably
     it rippled 'cross the floor.

The Lady of the House was called
     to find the tidal source.
Alas, it was no mystery,
     no need for Inspector Morse.
The master key she used
     to open up the room next door
and tentatively tiptoed in
     and started to explore.

Behind the shower curtain, starkers
   (she broke into a sweat),
Graham was warbling some song by
   who else but Wet, Wet, Wet.

The Lady of the House
   was almost overcome by shock,
with averted eyes she fumbled,
   found and turned off the stopcock.

So, Graham, next time you're minded to run
   hot water in your sink,
don't put the plug in, mate,
   or we'll all be in the drink.

The 'Little Bang' Theory

Pssst!

        Listen up. This is how it all began,
        way, way back before the dinosaur or Man,
        a concept called the Grand Design or Plan.

Pop!

        No-one was there to witness what came next.
        For centuries our best savants were perplexed,
        dismissed as stories Holy Scriptures' text.

Crack!

        So now imagine emptiness and space.
        All the Universe's mass in one small place.
        A theory must all facts and points embrace.

Plop!

        The start, 'Big Bang',
            a phrase coined by Fred Hoyle,
        rapid expansion, as if upon the boil,
        accelerating, till it may recoil.

Ting !

> If this were true, all would be black as night.
> In all this time, matter would be out of sight.
> Ergo, the bang was small, not big. I'm right?

Quite!

> Now the latest theory is 'dark matter',
> not one proposed by Wonderland's Mad Hatter,
> but seemingly backed up by all the data.*
> I'm off back to when the Earth was flatter.

* US pronunciation

__Ändamålet (I__ngvar __K__amprad, __E__lmtaryd, __A__gunnaryd, Sweden)

This poem is purpose built for your enjoyment.
You have chosen a poem which has been
ergonomically designed
by our team of experts
trained at the University of Gothenburg.

It is handcrafted, utilitarian, minimalist, modern,
but –
combines these features
with outstanding beauty and value for money:

Bauhaus as interpreted by Abba.

Simply open the pack and follow the instructions.
Assembly time: 15 minutes.

Should it fail to live up to your expectations
and our exacting standards,
contact our customer services.

Should any words be missing,
please contact our spares department.

poem x 2, team, experts, University, Gothenburg, features, beauty, value, money, Bauhaus, Abba, pack, instructions, assembly, time, minutes, expectations, standards, customer services, words, spares department

---

is x 2, built, have, chosen, has been, designed, live, trained, open, combines, interpreted, follow, should x 2, fail, contact x 2, be missing,

You, our x 4, it x 2, which

ergonomically, simply, please

by x 2, of x 2, at, with, for, as, to x 2,

this, purpose, the x 3, handcrafted, utilitarian, minimalist, modern, these, any, 15, your

but, and x 3

Trust Me – I'm a…

Election time is here again. I make promises galore.
Alas, they may be sacrificed when I
      speak from the floor.

Trust me, I'm a politician.

Pay tribute to the fallen on this extra special day.
I'll lay poppies from the front.
      From the rear I'll lead the fray.

Trust me, I'm a general.

Let me secure your future,
      ring fence your retirement plan,
I'll speculate in hedge funds, futures, bitcoins.
      I'm your man.

Trust me, I'm a financial adviser.

Aum. We all seek guidance in our journey on this earth.
I'll help you find your true self
      for I know how much you're worth.

Trust me, I'm a guru.

For a trifling, small percentage, say 1.5 to 2,
I'll watch your des. res. sell itself
        and charge the bill to you.

Trust me, I'm an estate agent.

Just take a seat upon the couch. To help me in my quest
to cast the role of Joan of Arc
        I'll have to see your breasts.

Trust me, I'm a casting director.

Hello! Hello! What have we here?
        Sports car? Midlife crisis?
I'm sometimes amnesiac depending what the price is.

Mind as you go, sir. I'm a speedcop.

Incurable? There's no such thing.
        Look at my plaque embossed.
Believe in me for I can cure...
        It may entail a cost.

Trust me, I'm a faith healer.

Amazing what a lab coat means.
        I'm erudite and smart.
From brushing teeth to climate change,
        I have a little chart.

Trust me, I'm a scientist.

Please open wide your mouth. Say 'Aaagh!'.
        Now slip your trousers off.
Just wait a moment while I cup my hand below.
        Now cough.

Trust me, I'm a doctor.

And last, not least and up to now
        forgotten in this rhyme,
I'm the investment banker
        who thought up a ploy subprime
that no-one understands
        but that guaranteed my bonus.
What financial crisis?
        You all share the common onus.
I'm a little more reluctant
        dividing up my spoils.
Give or take the odd mill.,
        I only cost the same as Royals.

Trust me? You'd have to be mad.

Good night. Farewell. Remember.
       Just maintain the status quo.
It's yours to put your faith in,
but in what is ours to know.

Trust us, we're the Establishment.

Drabble: 70+ (The Clock)

The body clock is ticking, sticking to its rhythm,
urgent, unforgiving, sieving out the dross.
Slyly, Time comes creeping, sweeping like a besom,
never ever slowing, knowing what is floss.

hectic, dramatic, frantic, traumatic,
drastic, kinetic, cryptic, splenetic,
plastic, bombastic, elastic, fantastic.

Tick, tick, tick. Tock, tock, tock.
Listen to that click. Listen to that clock.

Dad, at 70, dying, sighing did no good.
Finished all our weeping, peeping over shoulder
colder winds are blowing, flowing in the blood.
Precious Time is giving, living to be older.

Living to be older.
Getting ever older.
Getting ever older.
Tick, tick, tick

Drabble: Choices

It had been a long night.

As the patrol advanced, a pallid sun pierced the wispy haze of smoke hanging over the ruins of the farmhouse. The distant chatter of machine guns and sporadic whine of bullets kept them alert.

The corporal gestured to move forward one by one to where they overlooked the outskirts of the village.

A German soldier was shuffling slowly across the open ground, tired, wounded and demoralised, dragging his rifle. The corporal took aim, then lowered his own weapon. Their eyes met briefly.

In later years, Adolf and the corporal often reflected on that moment.

Drabble: Incident

11 o'clock and all's not well.

A pulsating blue floods the hallway
as I go to put out the bins,
part of the weekly domestic ritual.

A fire engine is blinking a warning
and the road is closed.
From a car's gaping bonnet, dense smoke
is rising towards the clear night sky,
where Perseid meteor showers are due.
I'll miss these as I did the windscreen
scattering its razor sharp confetti.
and the flames which roasted the neighbours' shrubs.

A lone figure, helmet and visor in place, douses,
observed from a distance. Overhead, ephemeral streaks
of space debris pass unseen.

Heroes and Supper Heroes

We're Snow Goose Supper Heroes.
       Our Bat Cave is upstairs.
We gather every second week
       in dribs and drabs and pairs.
Our witching hour is 8 pm.
       The current theme's unfurled.
We settle round the table
       and prepare to save the world.

With pints topped up and poems in hand
       to get the juices flowing,
which way the Muse will take us,
       there is no way of knowing.
Most weeks, it's Jude or 'SouzaMan'
       who gets the topic rolling.
Some nights, we'll chip in readily;
       some nights, we need cajoling.

We're wild. We're nonconformist:
       a heterogeneous bunch.
It may be nearly supper time, but us,
       we're out-to-lunch.
You will know us by our earnest tones
       or by our fervent rants.

We'll sweep you up with rhetoric.
>You may just think we're 'pants.'

There's Howard B., 'Dalmatian Man',
>whose side-kick's name is Ruby.
He'll puzzle you. She'll nuzzle you
>whilst each to each so true be.
His verse, by turns is stern and sharp.
>By turns it's quite romantic.
It's woven with such dainty skill,
>it's sexually tantric.

And Super Mark? It's not for wimps
>the way his shelves are stacked:
explosive, super critical, political, jam packed.
His delivery ferocious, controlled, not off his trolley.
You know he's rather unconstrained,
>though RADA trained, by golly!

We have our Supper Woman, too,
>goes by the name of Zoe.
She sprinkles us star dusted,
>Martian spiders just like Bowie.
There's Doug and me and Patrick P.
>It's really quite a shock.
We boldly goes, Star Trek heroes
>like Scotty, Kirk and Spock.

But our Supra Supper Heroes
        are the ones you least expect,
the quiet ones, the serious ones,
        whose words are weighed and checked.
They make their contributions
        (yes, it's Simon R. and Abbie).
And how I wish I had
        the turn of phrase of Scotland's Rabbie!
for as 'The best laid schemes
        o' mice an' men gang aft agley,'
our other Snow Goose heroes
        have at least 2 feet of clay.

Well, damn and blast, I'd meant to write
        of Columbines and Pierrots
and Harlequins, of Roman twins
        and Romes that burned whilst Neros
just fiddled on, a bit like me.
        We can't all be Shakespeare-os,
but do our best when whistle blows
        to have score lines of zeros.

Chorus Line Sonnet

These are but words which dance across the page,
each one entrusted with a minor role,
a chorus line, hands linked upon the stage,
recruited to the company's ensemble, whole,

to catch the eye, add meaning to the tale
where swans and maidens nightly interchange
or climax with a splits to make you pale
in feathers, basques and frilly costumes strange.

So, come, my little helpers, well-rehearsed,
convey this message verbatim expressed.
Perform the task at hand and be dispersed
and help me get this quickly off my chest.

Then whether pet or *recherché*, each word
takes flight, escapes, is gone, like youth's sweet bird.

Glimpsed I

Only a single decker,
but that extra height and the freedom
to observe and savour and capture
the random flashes of Autumnal suburbia
not accessible to the commuting driver,
allow me to peek over the boundary fence.
Through the protective netting, I glimpse
the square where once I hit a six off the last ball,
so uncharacteristic, so unexpected,
 not just by teammates, but by me.
I relive the glow and only half-remember,
suppress, another time, another day,
another side of the coin,
captaining the side to defeat
from a position almost invulnerable:
the tangible arctic *froideur*
of the dressing room post-match
still sends a shiver.
Now I'm the one who's hit for six.
For there, in the middle,
where bowlers hunt for rabbits,
is a sheep, single and singular,
cropping the hallowed turf.
The bus moves on, but the image
and my memories remain.

Glimpsed II

Let's go back to late summer.
On a bright, warm Sunday morning,
I come across the Knights' Trail and discover
an unknown side to Northampton: its history.
The helmeted, chain-mailed, halberd-bearing warriors
tower over me, their protective garb evolving
as the centuries pass: 11th, 12th, 13th...
I cower beneath their girth to read our past.
I head up the wooded slope of Castle Mound,
the path bordered with nettles, brambles, bottles and cans
and in the spotlighted clearing, I glimpse fluorescence.
Two bodies prone, stretched out, immobile.
Splendour in the grass.
They sport peaked caps, heavy coats
topped with brilliant jackets of primrose or amber.
My first thought is 'police', but the penny drops:
traffic wardens, napping in the sweltering heat.
I've disturbed their slumber.
The man gently wakes his mate and,
like startled cattle, they saunter off,
feigning insouciance and, though caught bang to rights,
in flagrante delicto, showing their human foibles,
they're back on duty. Motorists beware!
They're on the prowl and grumpy.

Glimpsed III

It was like seeing the Evening Star,
a lone beacon in the firmament,
but this was not night sky,
but daylight and suburban pavement.
Resting on the autumnal debris of the quiet cul-de-sac,
a polished jewel glinted back the sun,
its brilliant, gleaming, untarnished sheen
demanding my attention.
'Look at me!', it screamed.

Suddenly I'm aware the street is strewn
with tens of tiny metal canisters,
each blazing back the sun's rays, dazzling
reflected sunlight as from snow crystals,
or shiny seaweed on a pebbled strand,
a dusting of Christmas glitter under the tree,
the lights of an outback settlement,
a hamlet snuggled on a hillside.

I'm hyperventilating on images.
I'm sky high, euphoric,
as butaned out as last night's Bacchanalians
as I head off for the match.

Glimpsed IV – Perfect Timing

I pause before the portal
with its massive wrought iron gate,
and inscription, 'To the Fallen.'*
Beyond the cricket field, bristling,
vigorous green in the brittle sunshine,
the ancient stone buildings survey the scene
and another generation of bustling ephemera.

It's two days before May Day.
I catch a glimpse, a frozen, single frame shot,
of busy, white clad, frothy youngsters
and white jacketed, floppy-hatted umpires,
weighed down with their responsibilities
and the bulk of top pullovers tied
by sleeves round ample waists.

A change of bowler? Right arm over,
he flicks the ball with wristy exuberance,
three, four, five times and ambles in to launch
his missile towards the peak-capped adversary.
Down on one knee, the batsman clouts the ball
confidently away in my direction
with a terrific, satisfying thwack
which echoes back, amplified around the ground.

The little chap next to the square leg umpire
dives full length, holding the rocket
with consummate ease, a sweet, fumble-free peach,
like a cormorant smoothly piercing the deep
or a kestrel plummeting free-fall on to its prey.
I glimpse the catch,
a millisecond of memory imprinted, seared.
A raised finger, a wicket falls, and
a dispirited trudge to base for reinforcements ensues.

Head buzzing with past moments,
dollies and scorchers, some taken cleanly,
others bobbling but clutched or
squeezing from clumsy butterfingers,
dropped, chance given and gone.
I head for home and tea-time peace.

*The gate is actually inscribed:
 '1939-1945: Gate of Remembrance.'*

Glimpsed V – Feather: Turned Out Pessimistic Again

I remember a day or so ago
glancing by chance out the kitchen window,
pondering big questions (breakfast? weather?)
and watching, pirouetting down, a feather,
out of a clear sky, so graceful and slow:
a portent, a sign or just some mobbed crow?

Quill first it fell, a pivot for the plume,
a perfect spiral pathway did assume.
The quill wrote words ephemeral, unread,
ink invisible, yet an image sped
to memory's treasure house where it's stored
and filed amongst the precious, cluttered horde.

'Write better and write more for Time is short.
Even at a sprint you'll still be caught
mid-phrase by Death's impartial intervention.'
The falling feather had my whole attention.
It fluttered to the ground, was still, yet stirred
more introspection, more dark thoughts absurd.

Tonight, cascading feathers haunt each dream.
Too soon, tomorrow joins yesterday's long stream.

Glimpsed VI – Blackbird, Buzzard, Weasel, Bee, and the Mutant

The startled blackbird,
disturbed in its foraging amongst July's wild raspberries,
took to the air with an irascible scream of alarm
and a whirr of wings as we flew by on the bikes.

Not so the buzzard, disdainfully rising
with slow-motion, powerful flaps from roadside verge
to perch on lowest branch of adjacent oak,
weighing up for size
       the glinting morsels of its Lycra®-ed prey.

Unlike our fellow road users, we make no noise
and the juvenile weasel, crossing in airborne bounds,
 scurried to cover,
       not much fatter than a juicy quadruped worm,
an arrow flash of brown tail, body, forelegs.

Hidden amongst the climbing fronds,
       the pollinator lurked.
My hand, searching for full pods,
       found, not pea, but bee.

The surprise was mutual:
  painful for one, lethal for the other.
No bicarbonate could soothe the bee's fatal lesion.

The size of a sickly pigeon,
  it wandered amongst the shoppers.
This was no wagtail despite pied plumage.
Grey-brown, white-spotted breast,
  scavenged morsel in bill, mutant or mongrel,
cocked head and bold-eyed demeanour proclaimed,

'I am blackbird.'

Glimpsed VII – Wildebeest?

Friday lunchtime and a steady stream of traffic
flows along the smooth, black, fresh tarmac
towards the roundabout.
We bob along and, as we exit past
the central reservation, there he is,
like a vision from another world.
Had a wildebeest tentatively ventured
from the bank of its island refuge, pushed by the herd
past lunch-hungry, snapping crocs,
towards the watering hole on our left,
we could not have been more astonished.
Even a unicorn, brashly, boldly, brazenly,
crossing at a trot, would have left us
little more stunned, astounded.
With not a teeter nor the slightest vacillation
nor a glance in our direction,
the unicyclist, blasé with the knowledge
of youth's invulnerability, pedalled to the far side
and on his circumambulatory way.

Glimpsed VIII – Keeping a Little Something for Later

The apple tree grows at a crazy, gravity-defying angle,
just waiting for one of us to cry, 'Timber!'
It's laden once again with its juicy orbs
and we're here to collect fruit, not firewood.

We've soon harvested all we can reach,
teetering on tiptoes and at full stretch,
so it's time to make use of our step ladder,
ready for volunteer or pressed man
to totter rung by rung and tentatively lean,
parallel with the tree, to grasp each prize.

And there on the flat surface of a lower branch
sit the remains of a recent feast, squirrel munched,
freshly tooth-marked, put aside on his table
for a snack later in the gatherer day
to bridge that between meal gap
and calm those niggling pangs.

Thought for Today: A *Trumble*?

Today I sat down in my chair with a thump
and thought I would twitter like President Trump.
Each nocturnal, 140 character burst
would end with the phrase, 'America first.'

I'd smooth down my hair and curl up my lip
and give it out straight as I shoot from the hip.
I'd spit out invective and dollop out scorn
and make all those Muslims regret they were born.

I'd sign a decree to impose travel ban,
'cos foreigners by birth are un-A-merican.
I'd stab with my finger and screw up my eyes
and not even blink as I tell you more lies,
for lies don't depend on what once was called 'Truth'
and dissed by the liberal elite as uncouth.
If it's black and white striped and smells like a skunk,
but fits with your credo, you know it's not bunk.

Ladies, we love you, so don't be a dope.
You know that it's never for words that I grope.
Soon it's quite clear for who(m) I am rootin' :
first Donald J Trump, then Vladimir Putin.

I learned from my dad how to duck and to dive.
I'm 45th. President, Colt 45.
The Paris agreement corrodes our Rust Belt,
so I don't give a damn if both ice caps melt.

I'm all full of bile, xenophobia and hate.
Rally round, folks! Let's make America great!

Secret Valentine

It's that time of year again
to write a Valentine,
to find a biro or a pen
and ask you to be mine.
Perhaps I'll get my i-pad
and type a verse or three,
full of humour undergrad,
though I guess you'll guess it's me.

I'll pop it in an envelope
once Pritt®-stuck to a card.
I wonder if there's any hope
I'll be your 'V-day' bard?
So, sweetie, have you guessed yet
from whence these lines have come?
It's someone you've already met.
Give up? I'm keeping *schtum*.

Railroaded*

*Written in Sandy Milsom's Macclesfield Creative
Writing Group workshop in response to a photograph of
an engine driver standing in the cab of a steam
locomotive, looking back down the track.

It's a sad day, a sad day, a full head of steam,
flying along, flying along, pulls like a dream.
The gradient's gentle, but downhill all the way.
We've stoked up the fire. A very sad day,
on course for the future, electric and diesel,
with most of the lines closed, Beeching, you weasel!
We've spent a whole lifetime from station to station
and now we've reached our last destination.
Wave the flag. Blow the whistle. Enough is enough.
The steam age is over and we're right out of puff.

Typo: A Haiku-esque Three Line Quip

Holy mackerel!
Forecast is god for Sunday.
Another typo!

The Preservèd Village

After 'The Deserted Village' by Oliver Goldsmith

Sweet Beckley, loveliest village of the shire,
where working folk plan someday to retire,
where season follows season with a sport,
though 'Don't be optimistic', Life has taught,
where Oxford may be up, yet could go down,
Uniting all, though more town folk than gown.
Here, far from madding crowd or London's pomp,
the locals stroll through fields where Spring lambs romp
and savour village Life at walking pace,
a stone's throw from Brize Norton's airfield base.

Bucolic idylls sadly face the threat
of sudden change if bottom line's not met.
The village focal point, its vital hub,
its beating heart, its watering hole, the pub,
is central to a social unity
identifying each community.
is crucial for its daily Life to thrive,
the single means by which it can survive.
Thus, came to pass, despite its many charms,
the mooted closing of 'Th' Abingdon Arms.'

At once, a cry ran round that we must act.
Plans were conceived, unanimously backed.
The owners, Brakspeare, listened, but unmoved,
proposed a buy-out scheme and so it's proved
a mettle-testing project for our ties.
How many would respond to rallying cries?
But first the legal niceties were done
(and everyone's aware that that's no fun).
The enterprise conceived was firstly named,
its constitution then agreed, once framed.

Its officers were volunteered or pressed
to pledge their time and energies invest.
Some readily stepped up to others coax
with mild coercion, repartee and jokes.
Appeals were issued to take out a share
with fingers crossed, breath held, a wing and prayer.
The deadline fast approached to raise the sum,
two days to go and 40 k to come.
Some miracle perhaps would intervene.
It did. Job done by midnight, Hallowe'en.

The rest, my friends, we celebrate tonight.
Our venture's just beginning. Future's bright.
Support your local with your kin and friends.
Thus, it grows and prospers whilst my poem ends.

Solitude

After 'Daffodils' by William Wordsworth

I wandered lonely in a crowd
whilst posting thoughts unveiling ills.
I walked along and talked out loud -
Aren't earphones great! They're really brill -
beside the bank, through shopping malls,
whilst still online with website pals.

Continuous as the stars that tweet
or presidents at 4 am
their every thought quite indiscrete,
oh, how I do so envy them!
Ten thousand followers at a glance,
each logging on at every chance.

My Facebook® page where I lay bare
the trivia of each passing day
is where I live or simply stare
or turn to online games and play.
These habits steal my days. They filch,
so social intercourse is *zilch!*

For often on my couch, I lie
and nothing much comes on TV.
I sometimes ask myself just why
I am so cr*p at being me.
But then my heart with pleasure fills,
until I get my broadband bills.

The Build Up to the Let Down

After 'Slough' by John Betjeman

Come, friendly bombs, and fall on Howe,
on Tebbitt, Hurd: they're past it now.
They'd wheel out Thatcher (Holy Cow!)
were she not dead!
Come, votes, and blow to smithereens
the Coalition (not the Greens).
Make UKIP's zombie mob has-beens.
And what of Ed?

'This mess was left by Gordon Brown,'
says Gove, the miserable clown,
'And we have brought deficit down
in just 5 years.'
There goes that man with double chin
(and only Pickles' mind is thin).
It's others who apply the spin
brings us to tears.

Then there's that Paddy Ashdown bloke
hears exit polls and makes a joke.
'I'll eat my hat!' which he'll revoke
when tolls the knell.

Now unemployment's dropped a tad,
though Zero Hours will drive them mad.
Do they think eating's just a fad?
Go roast in Hell.

'It's tough to juggle lots of dough,
rent an address in Monaco
to keep one's income taxes low
or white be bled,'
whilst low paid workers bear the scars
and serve the drinks in caffs and bars.
But back to Huw's and Andrew Marr's
long night ahead.

Predictions come, predictions scare.
though Sunderland, first to declare,
sees Labour up, Lib Dems despair
and chew their nails.
Come, friendly bombs, no need to 'Pow!'.
Ed, Nick and Nige have all said, 'Ciao.'
The Tories rule the roost somehow
and greed prevails.

Now a PS: the SNP
swept Labour into misery.
Perhaps Scotland's the place for me?
So northward ho?
Tuition's free and NHS
's protected from that Osbourne jess.
Their monster's confined to Loch Ness.
5 years to go !

The 'Yellow Orrell' Sonnet: My Road Bike's Frame

After Sonnet 130 by William Shakespeare

My road bike's frame is nothing like the sun;
Coral is far more red than her rear light;
If toy tops spin, her wheels have scarcely spun;
If metal gleams, the mud her forks doth blight.
I've ridden cycle tracks seem smooth and wide,
But no such rides gives she for many weeks,
And though like attar scents, to nostrils glide
Her foetid lubricants, she makes faint squeaks.
I love to hear her spokes, as round they whirr,
Though music hath a far more pleasing sound.
Her gears may slip and make no cat-like purr.
On hills my road bike's treads cling to the ground.

And yet, sweet, steel-framed steed, my love's undimmed.
When up astride, I'm never heavy-limbed.

Loyalty (2019 edition)

I am a loyal subject of Her Majesty, the Queen.
This is subject to conditions.
Let me tell you what I mean.
Well, first of all, there's Phil the Greek.
He simply has to go,
returned to where he came from,
zone of drachma or euro.

Then that charlie, Charles,
who's spent a lifetime King-in-waiting,
never done a stroke of work
and is into tree-debating.
It's time for him to soil his hands
on pay that's minimum
and see how half the nation sweats
to put food in its tum.
I know he's getting on in years
and past retirement age,
but we all need a taste
of what makes up a 'living wage.'

So, Charles and his queen consort
could go part time at B and Q
and spend their days advising customers
where to find a screw,
while Harry, Wills and Kate
deliver papers door-to-door
or change nappies in a care home.
They'd find that quite a chore.

There's Edward, Andrew, Princess Anne,
the hangers-on abound.
 Add George and Charlotte to the list,
my head's spinning round and round.
And what about Prince Michael,
Dukes of Gloucester and of Kent:
it's time they did more than
cut ribbons and paid a decent rent.

And now I think about it, and it puts me in a tizz,
I'm no longer loyal to any royal, not even to Queen Liz.

Casey & Co's Roof

When gardeners come to Brookfield Lane
on days it happens not to rain,
they will have noticed recently
Casey and friends sat drinking tea,
delicious brew supplied by Pat,
which begs the question, 'Why is that?'
Don't be deceived. These lads don't shirk.
It's just a pause. They're hard at work.

This time the roof of shed-cum-shop
hung by a thread about to drop,
obliterating those inside
and risking gardener homicide.
So those who may anticipate
a follow-up to 'Casey's Gate,'
sit back whilst I relate my tale
(also available in braille).

How handy is our shed-cum-shop!
To buy our compost in we pop
and, queuing up in single file,
there's even service with a smile.
Our credit's good, but we pay cash
for pellets, lime, bone meal, potash.

And so it came as quite a shock
when leaky roof attacked the stock.

The dreadful news like wildfire spread.
Matters came quickly to a head.
Committee members met and frowned.
'We mustn't see our assets drowned.
Let's formulate an action plan.
As with that gate, Casey's our man.
To help he'll need a hand-picked crew,
(though almost anyone will do).

Step 1: dismantle rotten roof.
Step 2: make new one weatherproof.
Between Steps 1 and 2, Step 3:
make sure they don't run out of tea.'
Now Dave had recently retired
and in a flash found himself hired
and as his job he'd called a halt on
he gave a hand the roof to **BOLT ON**.*

Another vital wheel in t'cog,
was John man and his faithful dog.
John's canine chum would stand on guard
ensuring no-one worked too hard.

And so that it went smooth and slick,

our volunteers co-opted Mick.
One final ploy: Facebook® appeal
for more to come and share their zeal.

On the day, the gang assembled,
joists and rafters creaked and trembled.
The day of reckoning was nigh,
with blazing sun, the pressure high
and omens good for such a task,
a day more fit to bronze and bask.
But, first things first, the dirty bit:
demolish roof and curse and spit.

The valiant crew began to sweat,
their overalls showed patches wet
and throats were parched whilst foreheads dripped.
How come their morale hadn't dipped?
Thanks to Pat's kind ministrations,
meriting standing ovations,
a constant flow of tea they downed
with water for John's faithful hound.

That night when daylight's glow had fled,
 the precious stock in shop-cum-shed
was sheltered by a sturdy sheet,
protecting heaped up sacks of peat.
The blue tarpaulin firmly roped

with breeze and prowlers amply coped.
Now to the step requiring strength:
lift roof board cut to measured length.

Somehow our men in sapping heat
achieved this Herculean feat.
They pulled and puffed. It slowly rose
to where it was destined to pose.
At times, all four were up aloft.
This was no task for someone soft
or suffering from vertigo.
To heroes this new roof we owe.

Enough, my friends, it now remains
when you call in for bamboo canes,
to gaze, admire their work of art
and know that it came from the heart.
So there I'll end and draw a veil,
round off this warm, uplifting tale.
Forgive if I have waffled on
about Dave, Casey, Mick and John.

Let's raise the roof for Casey's saga:
3 rousing cheers and pints of lager.

* *Dave is an avid fan of Bolton Wanderers.*

<u>The Gardener's Butterfly Prayer</u>

O God, all-seeing, who is wise,
I love all graceful butterflies.
They float and feint and pose and rise;
each dart which gravity defies
an unpredictable surprise.
They are free spirits in disguise:
a balm, a lotion for the eyes.
Their wafting flight all sense denies.
Although diminutive in size,
of airborne insects, they're the prize.
(Think aphids, midges, wasps and flies).

O God, who all our sins espies,
ignore this guff, this pack of lies
for cabbage whites I just despise.
One cannot bear them, though one tries,
rejoicing when their species dies.
Why they exist reason defies.
I plot to bring on their demise.
You will not stop me with your sighs
or tempting me with thoughts of thighs.
I wish it could be otherwise.
I must, alas, prioritise.

O God, please help me fight the fight.
Yes, I despise the cabbage white.
Exterminate the little shite.
They seem to take such great delight
when on my sprouts and greens alight
and though they dance and twirl in flight,
for me they are a dreadful blight
upon the earth, so much I might
take measures to resolve my plight:
invent a gadget causing fright;
robotic arm which swipes from height;
train some insectivores to bite;
or build some traps which squeeze them tight.

I wouldn't be the least contrite
for the reaction they incite.
It's evil, yes, for it's not right
on helpless bugs to vent one's spite.
Alas, this is a qualm so slight
I try to kill all those in sight.
I'd work until it's almost night
to clear the last one from our site.

Perhaps the future would be bright
if they could join the trilobite,
a specimen by Araldite®
fixed on a slide like lymphocyte
and viewed by a revealing light
by pupil, prof. or acolyte,
a thing of study recondite.

      O, God, destroy the cabbage white!

                Amen.

Frenzy: Where There's Muck, There's Brassica*

The delivery arrived in the morning
when the load was expected and planned
and some took to heart the forewarning
and made sure that their garden was manned.

The pile had had scarce time to settle.
Wisps of steam were just starting to rise.
Each gardener was put on his mettle,
actions springing from words to the wise.

Each was armed with fork, sacks and barrow,
these zealots who were first on the scene,
disappearing up paths long and narrow.
The heap visibly shrank where they'd been.

They stuck to their task with a vigour.
Six barrowsful was the quota assigned,
though whether applied with a rigour,
let's just say I've an eye which is blind.

Like a shimmering mirage in heat haze
or a liquid spread out in the sun,
one minute a towering hill's in your gaze,
you blink twice and the next it has gone.

The dung beetle's known for its penchant,
gathering up what it treats as pure gold,
ignoring what others call stench and
trundling it off before it grows cold.

We've a similar outlook, we gardeners.
We see value in animal waste.
Gung-ho with dung, O don't be hard on us.
Our produce will be more to your taste.

** Poetic licence: in fact, manure is best avoided for the
brassica bed.*

Dave and Casey

If you call at our allotment and wonder how we keep
the place so neat and tidy, it's two men who never sleep.
They're constantly on duty, if appearances are right
and I reckon that they sometimes even
      camp there overnight.
You will not need three guesses
      to name these fine, upstanding men.
It's Dave and Casey, Siamese twins.
      You'll find them in their den.

They've overhauled the bunker
      and they've built a new raised bed.
They laid the bricks and mortar
      till the poor sods' fingers bled.
They filled it up with topsoil
      and Dave's wife did the rest.
With marigolds and dahlias and tomatoes
      we're now blessed.
The shop front was quite grotty,
      so they took the time to pave
with slabs and stone one of them sourced.
      Was it Casey or our Dave?

You' ll have seen them trimming hedges
   and carting to the tip
every leaf and twig and branch
   they were obliged to clip.
They gathered up scrap metal
   which had lain around the patch
and flogged it off at Henshaw's
   who found he'd met his match
for Casey bargained for best price.
   He had Henshaw in tears,
but with that Glo'ster burr he said,
   'Thanks very much, my dears.'

They've seeded near the raised bed
   to give that crowning touch.
They're running out of projects.
   At straws they'll start to clutch.
Perhaps we're overdue a bar
   where we could quench our thirst,
once weeding duties over.
   It would likely be a first.
One thing is sure and certain.
   We don't need a sauna or a gym.
We dig at speed and hoe and weed
   to keep ourselves in trim.

And now I've sung their praises
       in these verses sweet and short.
I speak for every one of us
       in offering our support.
 So, when you see them in the shop,
       tidying up those nooks,
buy your compost bags and smile
       and maybe buy my books*!
Keep up the good work, Casey.
       Dave, don't **Wander**** off too far.
What a brilliant partnership!
       Let's just end with one big 'Ta!'

* *Unashamed plug for 'Eric Bloodaxe? And Other Verse', 'Seconds Out', 'Lifelines' and 'BLAA, BLAA, Black Sheep'. As with all my poetry booklets, proceeds go to* **Prostate Cancer UK.**

** *Yes, this is he, Dave, the avid fan of Bolton Wanderers, as encountered here in an earlier Occasional poem.*

Working Party Time

Not another bloomin' ditty from
        that bloomin' Poyser bloke.
You can't sneeze up here without some verse.
        It's getting past a joke.

October 10th. we'd mobilised
        the Autumn working party
with every chance we'd finish up
        all sweaty, tired and clarty.
At 10 o'clock, we've got stuck in
        with tasks explained to t'work force,
with Mick's lot at the far end
        where Casey's bantering till he's hoarse,
whilst Dave's team clears hedge cuttings
        from a plot that's overgrown
along with Graham the Treasurer,
        so not quite on his own.

Then Phil poles up and joins them
        to shred trimmings for the tip
and it takes a good 10 minutes
        ere Dave has to crack the whip.

They're chatting about cricket, Brexit,
        what crops have failed this year
and just how long it seems till t'break
        and will there be some beer.
But somehow Dave's trailer gets filled
        right to the brim and cuttings stashed,
but there's lots of work remains to do
        before the tea gets mashed.
It's like those digs you see with
        Tony Robinson on TV
except it's much more frenzied,
        barrows buzzing past you– one – two – three.

There's Maggie with a shovel
        shifting shavings in a blur
and Mick, Big Bob and Jane's mum
        struggling to keep pace with her.
It's a triumph for our teamwork
        and when the dust cloud clears,
the space is rough and ready,
        gone accumulation of the years.

So, the chips are down or rather up,
        sweats trickling down our backs.
A kettle's boiling on the grill
        between the sheds and shacks.
The tea is brewed. It's sipped and slurped
        with great enthusiasm
and more than one of us seize up
        with cramp and muscle spasm.

Sausage rolls we scoff and sponge cake
        worthy of 'Great British Bake Off'
and we're a little bit rebellious
        when it comes to t'time to break off,
but back we go to finish off
        the task we have in hand
knowing our allotment site's improved.
        It surely will be grand,
but one of us has lost the plot
        or rather lost his keys
and spends the next two days
        around the site upon his knees.

Phil's fervent prayers are granted
        just as all hope's begun to fade.
They're found at home in Mady's bag!
        Not lost, merely M/s-laid.

Just two more lines still to recite,
        then I'll get back to my beer.

That sponge cake! Those sausage rolls!
        When's working party time next year?

The Blackberry Jam Scandal

It's been quite a while since I wrote you an ode
on Brookfield Allotment and what our folk showed
and which veg won prizes and whose faces glowed
a whole year ago at the annual fête.
I've written of noticeboards, shop roof and gate –
so, it's time that I gave you another update.

Well, next to the flower bed, we now have a bench.
You can sit – if you've time – at the risk of a drench,
with plenty of room for yourself and your wench.
It's raised on a platform of stout paving stones,
assembled by Dave and, of course, Casey Jones
and what better place to play *Game of Thrones*.

That flower bed is worthy of prizes at Tatton.
You get a good view from the bench that you're sat on
unless garden fatigue has you lying out flat on.
There are dahlias with heads as big as a plate,
creeping nasturtiums that are good when they're 'ate'
and too many others for me to relate.

And this year's show was a roaring success.
Now I'll come to my title which I should address
and my lack of first prizes which caused some distress*.
With *Single Sweet Pea*, I walked off with second prize.
There were at least three exhibits. I tell you no lies,
but it's on jams and jellies that I'd set my eyes.

Two jars of each I entered, hoping not to be bested,
but these categories were hotly contested.
and it's only now my disappointment has festered.
The white currant jelly was a bit out of left field
and the redcurrant sadly was scarcely congealed.
My first jam – nothing – for imminent failure I steeled.

With blackberry jam unopened, my Fate was sealed.
Perhaps I was unlucky. Maybe it was the gamble
of mislabelling the d$mn thing, blackberry, not bramble?

Not really!

'Slugging' it out in No Man's Land

The twilight hour: it's now or never;
over the top and time to attack.
The terrain's wet. It's perfect weather.
We'll hit them hard and set off back.

The light is fading. Switch head-torch on;
weapons are ready and so are we.
We'll hunt them down till we've left none.
Then home to bed with the plot slug free.

Between you and me,
unfortunately,
this is a very,
quite temporary
valedictory
pseudo-victory.

Bang to Rights: Mayday, Mayday, Mayday*

Each of us lives a reality soap
and daily we follow the script.
We stride right along a treacherous slope
in which misadventures are slipped.

There's one of these tales that I want to relate.
You may think that I've lost the plot.
It happened in March (I've forgotten the date)
after into hot water I'd got.

At the allotment. I'd worked up a sweat.
To come clean, I needed that shower.
Whilst I'm not the sprucest that you've ever met,
still 'Cometh the Man, comes the scour.'

I'd washed and I'd rinsed and was ready to go.
I'd scrubbed up gleaming, right proper.
I was drying the walls so fungi don't grow.
It was then I came a right cropper.

I reached to my left. My feet slid to the right.
I must have leant over too far.
A bike on black ice is a similar plight -
though not ending under a car.

My head struck the side of the bath with a bang.
A right blinking wallop it gave me.
I didn't see stars, but bells echoing rang;
no chance to put hands out to save me.

It's had some ad-**verse** effects, you might say.
My eyesight has deteriorated,
but for a whole month, with words I couldn't play,
which folk here may think should be fêted.

It's said that each cloud has a lining 'argent.'
From each mishap we ought to learn.
But what lesson there is from a head with a dent,
I'm buggered if I can discern!

*The title nods to the day I wrote this poem – having
recovered from the effects described – 1ˢᵗ May, 2017.*

D-Day, Jour-J

June the 6th was D-Day way back in 1944,
when Allied troops disembarked
        on Europe's bloody shore
and France's liberation began the day they call Jour-'Jee'
and many a soldier lost his life that day in Normandy.

So, whether your name was Hans, my boy,
        or Jean-Pierre or Tom,
it's History repeated a stone's throw from the Somme.

The five pronged thrust from Neptune
        was planned to make a breach.
They came from Canada's wheat belt
        to die on Juno beach,
whilst Yanks who left the mid-West,
        home states both near and far,
perished under machinegun fire at Utah and Omaha.

So, whether your name was Hans, my boy,
        or GI Joe or Tom,
it's History repeated a stone's throw from the Somme.

The Brits were asked to play their part
        at Gold Beach and at Sword
to establish a bridge head in Operation Overlord,
but mothers grieve on both sides
        having lost their pride and joy
for *Lebensraum*'s worth nothing
        when it takes away your boy.

So, whether your name was Hans, my boy,
        or Fritz or Franz or Tom,
it's History repeated a stone's throw from the Somme.

Yes, it's History repeated
        a stone's throw from the Somme.

Clinging to the Wreckage

With thanks to John Mortimer, source for the title

I wake in the morning and lie there in bed,
mull over the thoughts running round in my head.
There's a twinge in my calf, a wheeze in one lung.
I'm sure it was different back when I was young.

I remember how peaceful and soundly I slept.
I'd close my eyes tight and at once I was swept
into a realm where wild fantasies reigned.
Sleep recharged the batteries. Now I'm just drained.

When I rise from my armchair, I hear someone groan.
Now who made that noise when I'm here on my own?
Then I let out a sigh. There's a creak in my knee.
I've a full repertoire of sounds deep inside me.

An orchestra's waiting for me to conduct
my very own solo in which tendons are plucked.
My organs are played in soprano or bass.
Sometimes there's surprise or relief on my face.

Ingestion's a problem. Digestion's more indi'
with results which can best be referred to as windy.
I burp like a baby and in that respect,
in this second childhood, I'm already wrecked.

Next thing I'll be wearing an incontinence pad.
I'd never have thought that when I was a lad.
I always imagined I'd be carefree and happy,
not frightened of laughing and sporting a nappy.

It's not a state secret that I am disclosing.
Like Bach and Beethoven, I'm now decomposing.
Sans teeth and sans hair, slowly falling to bits,
I share this in common with all the old gits.

Young Man, so disdainful, there's no time to scoff.
5 minutes from now, it's your turn to nod off
and then when you wake up, well, what a surprise!
Overnight you've adopted your father's disguise.
Girls, don't feel smug and look down on your brothers.
A blink of the eye and you've turned into your mothers.

Stigma of the Dumps

The black dog, the black dog, is curled up
       round my brain.
The black dog, the black dog, is driving me insane.
He's been howling and growling and prowling
       since my teens,
quaffing and scoffing my hydroxytryptamine.
He's lurking in my synapses, hungry for blood.
He makes me feel I'm worthless, that I'm
       no bloody good.
He's the Cerberus to my id. He slavers and he drools
and he can't be house-trained and won't
       put up with fools.
Am I barking mad you ask? You are so damned right!
I tread very carefully as bark may turn to bite.

Listen. Can't you hear them, the voices in my head?
They're cackling and whispering,
       'You're better off dead.'
I'm *out of work.* I'm *divorced and* I'm *often pissed.*
Roger M., you're spot on –
       I *aimed low in Life and missed.*
The skies are grey and overcast and wisps swirl round.
I'm the man who found a penny but lost a pound.

My soma's in a coma. My psyche's shrunk to nil.
Like old Spike's epitaph, 'I told you I was ill.'
At an all time low ebb, Life could not be bleaker.
It puts another slant on 'asylum seeker.'

The Samaritans have a help line. I must phone in.
I have to act, but I can't act. It's my serotonin.
Everything's an effort. I'm a walking neurosis.
I have a kind of psycho-osteoporosis.
It's not just being down and sad.
        It's more than just the blues
and it's not helped one bit by mixing pills and booze.
My nights are spent in turmoil. I grab an hour's sleep
eaten up by angst. It's enough to make me weep.
My days stretch out, one long, somnambulistic dream
with every now and then of hope a sliver of a gleam.

February 9th, 1929

If Sir Alexander Fleming had been a tidy worker
(and spent less time staring out the lab,
      though he never was a shirker) ...

If he'd neatly cleared away all his piles of Petri dishes,
we wouldn't have a drug to cure our epidermal fissures.

He left out his agar cultures which got
      cross contaminated
with a grey-green mould and this
      Gram + exterminated.*

Round the mould the gel was clear,
      which struck him as quite thrillin'.

Staph. aureus was scuppered.

      Eureka! Penicillin!

*Gram + (pronounced Gram plus) refers to Gram
positive bacteria*

Germinal: March 21st

There's a spring in my step, a sparkle in my eye.
Spare me half a minute and I'll tell you just why.
I'm not the sort of bloke who yearly goes bonkers
for Autumn's mellow yellows
      with chestnuts and conkers.
I might warm to the flame that fresh snow engenders
but it soon turns to slush, so I turn to 'East Enders'.

I can just about cope with heat waves 'cos they're rare,
but not livid pink of that sun-scorched flesh bare.
With that, like today, back to March 21st.
If you're still bearing with me, you're over the worst,
for the gleam in my eye and the bounce in my gait
are caused by these wonders I'm about to relate:

Spring's herald, the snow drop, first snaps into focus,
is very soon followed by gaudy, brash crocus.
Then tall, jaunty daff and self-conscious narcissus,
each nods its head skywards in frustrated kisses.
The catkins, precocious, lets dangle lambs' tails
which toss to and fro in the blustering gales,

whilst shy pussy willows its pollen provides
to impoverished bees as they search the hedge-sides.

In neighbouring fields, frisky lambs in their pairs
bleat, run up to suckle
            once Mum's checked they are hers.
It's too soon for the round-bellied cows to give birth,
but it won't be long now from the size of their girth.

The hawthorns are budding.
            There's a faint haze of green.
Through the brown of the ploughed fields,
            winter corns not yet seen.
The dawn chorus is strengthened by migrants' return,
yet deep in our hearts it's for swallows we yearn.

Now that Spring's here, we'll put forward the clocks.
Roll out the green carpet. Vernal equinox!

Dates: Figure This

2 - 4 - 6 - 8 - ... - ... - ... here's a thought to contemplate:
next in this arithmetic series, what's the date?

For 1 - 3 - 5 - 7 - ... - ... - ...
       here's my answer: Nine Eleven

It's Tuesday, early afternoon, about 2-ish GMT.
We're in the office, grafting hard
       or just passing time, maybe.
On Graham's desk, he has a screen
       which all day's illuminated
and brings hot press the latest news,
       so he's constantly updated.

And then he calls me over.
       Something odd has happened in the States
There's been a plane crash –
       'Strangest thing!' – the commentator insinuates.
'It's flown into the north tower
       of the World Trade Centre building.'
We take this with a pinch of salt.
       He's just the lily gilding.

It must be small – a private jet? –

       and we assume the guy's insane.

We're casually dismissive until it happens once again.

Now we really pay attention.

       What the hell is going on?

Then we can't believe our senses

       when we see the south tower's gone.

A real life drama is unfolding,

       History's happening as we gaze.

The whole world is in awe and shock.

       The whole world's in a daze.

As we watch, the second tower crumbles

       like sand castles on the beach

and suffocating clouds of debris

       come rolling from the breach.

Rubber-necking's over,

       spectators scatter, fearing for their lives.

Inside last words are shouted into phones

       by mothers, husbands, wives.

Some 3000 workers perished and 350 firemen too.

and all the people on 4 planes,

       passengers, terrorists and crew.

So is this where it all went pear-shaped, where
        Apocalypse drew near,
where America and Britain opened
        Pandora's box of fear?
Bush and Blair together went
        Desert Storming through Iraq.
It's been a downward spiral since
        and the clock can't be turned back.

Obama's been and gone since then
        and with him common sense.
Trump's in charge, a dreadful thought.
        There's no sitting on the fence.
Bin Laden's dead and Saddam too.
        Now Kim il Jong is raving,
provoking with his missile tests.
        For an earlier time, we're craving.

So fingers crossed and holding breath,
        at the slightest straw we clutch.
We yearn to live to tell the tale and say,
        'Thank you very much'.
The clock approaches midnight
        when all Life on Earth's extinct
We so stupidly played chicken!
        Which of us was it first blinked?

Dali's Moustache Limerick

Salvador Dali, surreal artist,
on his genius would always insist,
but is he Dada or Daddy
via an affair that he had? He
gives his Life and moustache one more twist.

Getting My Act Together – M-A-Y?

I watch James May dismantle
the turntable with a mixture
of childish wonder and dis-may.
The myriad, intricate entrails
dismembered, lie exposed in orderly patterns,
like with like, ready to reassemble
in a precise, logical way I know is beyond me.

My inner D-I-Y-er d-i-y-ed still born,
miscarried, ectopic, unnourished,
the three ply wires, red, brown and blue,
an umbilical cord strangling the nascent desire
to get back in the groove, to see a Phoenix rise,
to hear music rattle the rafters.

Lip Service*

'You can**not** be serious!', was his spoilt brat battle cry.
'That ball was in. You must be blind
　　　　or a very stoopid guy!'

Back then, line calls were made
　　　　on a simple puff of chalk,
but now technology has given us the eye of hawk,
whilst McEnroe has mellowed
　　　　and from commentators' box,
he gently criticises and occasionally mocks
this generation's mavericks, incompetents and worse,
shows mild surprise when Djokovic
　　　　is overheard to curse!

*Written in the second half of my Macclesfield Creative
Writing Group workshop on 'Tennis'.*

Limerick for Bardy: Post-Todmorden Goodbyes

Dedicated to the memory of our good friend
Barbara 'Bardy' McNair
18th November, 1949 to 28th May, 2017

Consideration, kindness, compassion,
Bardy had so much more than her ration
and the plain, simple fact is,
it was put it into practice
as if it were going out of fashion.

A Hymn to Home*

From North Sea to Atlantic vast,
from Dover's cliffs and Beachy Head
to Scotland's northern shores, from mast
we fly our flag, blue, white and red.

One people and one nation proud,
our borders now reclaimed and whole,
together we are all endowed,
O little island, great of soul.

Weather fronts and jet stream's wiles
have formed our temperament benign.
We shrug off daily tests and trials,
believe that all will turn out fine.

Our politicians selfless are
and our police are pure at heart.
Our health system's the best by far
compared to those in foreign parts.

We've made the world a better place
because of Britain's glorious past.
We've given English as a base.
and to tradition we hold fast.

We love our Queen. Long may she reign.
We've Lords and Crufts and Wimbledon.
On foreigners we pour disdain.
It's they we Brits look down upon.

So, hush, Remainers, hold your peace.
We've led you out, like knights of old,
from Brussel's grasp. Be not like Greece
impov'rished, but enriched and bold.

The Future's bright outside EU.
We will succeed against the odds.
We'll thrive. A golden era's due.
The choice is ours. The will is God's.

**Written in my Macclesfield Creative Writing Group
'New National Anthem' workshop. I have adopted a
voice and expressed views that are by no means mine.*

Resistentialism*

'Here he comes, Mr Fingers and Thumbs,
plonks himself down in our chair.
He's no idea, with his technophobe fear,
what he will access and where.'

Computer says, 'Just how many ways
are there to have him freak out?
So, old Keyboard, let his efforts be flawed,
till he fills with self-loathing and doubt.'

'He's scratching his head. (He'll wish he were dead
the moment he touches my keys).
Now he's started, two ticks and he's martyred.
We'll soon have him down on his knees.

Extra lettered, reversed and unfettered,
with errors and typos galore,
he'll gnash his teeth, loll his tongue underneath,
but tomorrow he'll be back for more.'

*Written in Simon Robinson's workshop on
relationships between inanimate objects and people.*

'Resistentialism' was coined by Paul Jennings and attributed to the fictitious philosopher, Pierre-Marie Ventre, whose school of philosophy was based on the concept that inanimate objects are spiteful: 'Les choses sont contre nous.' ('Things are against us.')

Lamb in a Box

At the farm shop, there was no-one behind the till,
but as I set down my basket,
she straightened up, clutching a baby's bottle.
I mumbled something I deemed appropriate,
eliciting peals of laughter.
'It's not mine', she grinned. 'It's a lamb.'
There in its cardboard box, wobbling on spindly legs,
just hours after being rejected,
separated from mother and twin and
with all its short Life's challenges ahead,
the newborn looked from surrogate to me and back.

'I've never been this close to something so young,'
I said, overlooking my daughter's birth.
'I have. I've seen them really close up,'
the man behind me laughed. 'I was a slaughter man.'

Outside the temperature dropped, the wind rose
and a harsh mix of hail and rain slapped down.

I stroked the lamb's head, felt a buzz of warmth
towards the newborn and the world in general,
picked up my carrier bag and headed home
with my steak pie, sausages, and marinated lamb chops.

Leviathan

It was beached on the shingle of our drive,
belly up, a monstrous fish out of water,
a bloated leviathan, innards spilling
from a gaping wound in its side.
But where had it come from?
How had it washed up there?

The mattress appeared one morning,
sprawled in the lee of the car, limp and incongruous,
a huge question mark billowing over its origins.
As we soon discovered,
it was not the council's problem –
so, we held a council of war,

ferried it to the tip
in our improvised hearse
and tossed it onto a sea of household flotsam
under which it would slowly sink without trace,
though more fitting surely would have been
a final resting place on the seabed.

Mark My Words Limerick*

There was a young man from Montmartre
who read books by de Beauvoir and Sartre.
'Let me tell you!' said he –
'All is calamity,
and the World's a total disâtre.'

*Adapted from Mark Henderson's 'Limerick instantané',
written at the Petersgate Tap, Stockport where I was
Guest Poet.*

Mine: O Mine Papa*

When pithead wheels still turned each shift
to drop the cage and then to lift
the colliers from their daily graft,
a mile deep buried down a shaft,
each man was 50 years condemned,
with two short weeks to rest and mend.

Chorus:
Repose and convalesce from earning
for the sunlight daily yearning.
Digging coal required no learning,
back when the nation's home fires burned
and our satanic mill wheels turned
before our mining jobs were spurned.

Both my granddads, dad and brother,
all the family save our mother,
uncles and cousins, neighbours too,
they shovelled coal the whole day through
or all the afternoon or night,
lit by a headlamp's ray of light.

Chorus:
Repose and convalesce from earning etc.

Their lungs were clogged up with coal dust.
They sweated cobs and swore and cussed.
Back up on top, they'd wash t'muck off
and smoke a Woodbine®, hack and cough,
and breathe the air, so fresh, so sweet
and feel the grass beneath their feet.

Chorus:
Repose and convalesce from earning etc.

Our sweat shone black for old King Coal.
He had us body, mind and soul,
but for our kids we wanted better.
Education could unfetter.
Down the pit they won't belong,
just sing about our lives in song.

Chorus:
Repose and convalesce from earning
for the sunlight daily yearning.
Digging coal required no learning,
back when the nation's home fires burned
and our satanic mill wheels turned
before our mining jobs were spurned.

*Inspired by Bob Fox's Guest Night at the Dog and
Partridge, Bollington, 2017. A sung version has been
recorded by Dave Clark to the tune of the traditional
song 'Penny Wager'.

'I Wanna Be a Proper Poet!' Blues

At the Bollington Boat and Folk weekend,
I heard a proper poet read.
Her verse had the 'oomph' to which I pretend,
that certain something which I need.

I.

I wanna be... I wanna be Jo Bell,
Canal Laureate, proto Prix Nobel.
Her verse is fun. It's entertaining
and brings the sun out when it's raining.
Like narrow boats, well built and crafted,
the end result of hours grafted:
of boaters and mallard chavs she'll tell.
I wanna be... I wanna be Jo Bell.

II.

I wanna be... I wanna be John Lindley.
Compared to his, my verse is spindly,
transparent, thin, inconsequential.
His is tight, each word essential
and whether serious or funny,
it's sharp and witty, on the money.
He wouldn't grope for rhymes like Swindley.*
I wanna be... I wanna be John Lindley.
As in Leonard Swindley (Coronation Street)

III.

I wanna be... I wanna be Joy Winkler.

an image conjurer, word tinkler.

'Town' and 'Lightning...', her verse dramas:

they're - what's that Ian Dury phrase? - yes, brahmas.

Her metaphors fly off the page

in rainbow colours, never beige.

Again I'm struggling. The rhyme's a 'stinkler'.

I wanna be... I wanna be Joy Winkler.

IV.

I wanna be... I wanna be Mark Rawlins,

so in your face, sometimes appallin',

political, direct, committed,

His stuff is oral, never twittered.

He rants. He snorts. It's from the heart.

It's biting satire, true and tart.

He'll give you a right old maulin'.

I wanna be... I sometimes am Mark Rawlins.

V.

I wanna be... I wanna be Nick Degg.
Comic, serious, off the peg.
He loves his football, abhors cricket,
tells fans of latter where to stick it.
He does accents, twists, surprises.
stick-up incompetents devises,
of Stoke and potteries gives a gleg.
I wanna be... I'd love to be Nick Degg.

VI.

I wanna be... I wanna be Helen Kay.
As delicate as eggshells the poems she'll lay.
She writes of chicken romance in the coop,
the strutting cock, whose crest will never droop,
the hen-pecked underchick who, as a ghost,
comes back to see that she's now Sunday's roast.
Her touch is light. There's poignancy, word play.
I wanna be... I wanna be Helen Kay.

VII.

I wanna be... I wanna be Holbrook, M.
She's the tops, the *crème de la crème*.
She writes short stories, poems and plays.
Her creative flair leaves others in a daze.
Loads of events she organises
and still has time to pick up prizes.
For every genre, she turns out a gem.
I wanna be... I wanna be Holbrook, M.

VIII.

I wanna be... I wanna be Jude D'Souza.
When he's not showing films down at the boozer,
he writes verse where terse
      internal rhymes are interspersed
and flow so naturally you burst to know
      who'll spot it first.
He sometimes shocks with anglo-saxon words that pluck
and twang your nerves, but only if essential.
      I'll pass the buck.
He's erudite and clinical. He's not a loser.
I wanna be... I wanna be Jude D'Souza.

IX.

I wanna be... I wanna be Luke Wright.
His images jump out and bite.
Word torrents flash from centre stage.
You'll race to read them on the page.
What's that? The sound of teeth being gnashed
Post '97, the dreams were trashed.
New Labour was just Tory-lite.
I wanna be... could never be Luke Wright.

I want to be a proper poet.
Oh, stop this whining. Shut it! Stow it!

What I need's an operation:
brain transplant, rejuvenation
to smooth the wrinkles in my verse.
Hmmm. Is this maybe even worse?

Every hour, each day, I'll keep trying.
By the seat of pants, I'm flying.
I want to make you sigh, amuse,
write poems of many shades and hues.

Sometimes there're rhymes, or verse that's free
and I'm almost happy being me.

Firing Blanks

Inside the envelope is another
and in that, a greetings card.

Two sunflower eyes, a plum tomato nose.
Two red pimentos generate the SMILE.

The card is blank,
but its message radiates loud and clear.
'Spread a little sunshine. Pass it on.'

Today, here it is again for you.
Inside the envelope is another
and in that, a greetings card...

Mount Rushmore: Faces to the Wind

(Visit to Cartmel to eat at L'Enclume, May 2015)

4 Presidential faces stare unmoved,
immortalised, idealised, improved,
the keystones of their generation,
the founding fathers of their Nation.

They oversaw the birth and growing pains.
They slowly cast aside the slavers' chains,
were savvy statesmen first and warriors last,
aware that Future's roots grew from the Past.
Determinedly they made and clinched the deal.
They talked the talk and sometimes stooped to *spiel*.

Perhaps right now somewhere in South Dakota,
plans are afoot on adding to the quota,
a frightening thought, set on Mount Rushmore's hump,
that curling lip, that sneer of Donald Trump.

Meanwhile upon our front room sideboard stands
a family photo: a group of 5 withstands
a raging gale's attempts to hurl them back.
Through gritted teeth, they grimace, wince from thwack,
our famous five, their faces fixed and still
upon that exposed spot, that Cumbrian hill.

To Washington, Jefferson, T. Rooseveldt
and Abe this national accolade heart felt
was carved and in that landscape, I can see
Hugo, Laura, Estelle, Mady and me.

Maundy Thursday / Jueves Santo

'Enjoy your Last Supper,' was all the text said.
Jesús couldn't get those four words out of his head.
He'd ordered the water. He'd ordered the tapas,
with olives from the Mount and plenty of *papas*.

He'd do the old trick of water to *vino*
and then they'd tuck into a right stonking beano.
There'd be a paella *à la mamma mía*
and one of his mates would sing 'Ave María'.

It would all be so scrumptious they'd never forget,
but that 'Last Supper' text
       brought him out in cold sweat.

The taverna had laid out the table upstairs.
and his mates arrived singly, in groups and in pairs.

Jesús looked at all twelve, but he couldn't decide
which one was hinting at imminent homicide.
'*Buen provecho!* What we're about to receive…',
Then, hey presto, they'd wine.
       Had he more up his sleeve?

To a clatter of plates, Pedro raised his glass in a toast.

He pushed back his chair saying,
      'Here's health to our host!'
Jesús leant towards him,
      squeezed his hand once or twice.
'Before the sun's dawning,
      you'll deny knowing me thrice.'

Pedro was shocked. He'd give his life for this man.
He considered himself Jesús' number one fan.

Jesús looked round benignly at the gathered throng.
'30 pesetas it's Thomas, though maybe I'm wrong
and Jude's looking furtive there, sandwiched between
Jaime and Juan. I wonder where he has just been.'

'You're pale and you're sweating.
      Come, let me cool your brow.
I'm a dab hand at healing as you'll soon avow.
Here we are in Galicia, good friends round the table.

Some think me a doctor, but I shrug off the label.'
The evening passed quickly. Jesús said, 'Adios'
Eleven mates were puzzled, didn't foresee their loss.
But the twelfth one knew he'd sold leader and friend
for a handful of silver which he couldn't defend.

Acknowledgements

First and foremost is Mady, who has managed to put up with me for three decades, through thick and thin, in full time employment and in retirement and even whilst I was in the throes of getting something resembling the right words in something resembling the right order.

Next is Charles 'Charlie' Heathcote, prolific author and creator of (our) Doris Copeland, without whom this pamphlet would not have seen the light of day. Charlie also suggested the front cover illustration, which precisely conveyed the concept I had in mind.

In addition to Charlie, sincere thanks are also due to authors Margaret Holbrook, Joy Winkler and Mark Henderson who have taken time from their own writing to read through these poems and give me feedback. And to my daughter, Paula Aamli, herself a sometimes-poet, who supported me by preparing this collection for publication.

Recognition of the part Macclesfield Creative Writing Group has played in supporting and encouraging me cannot be overstated.

Our workshops (Macclesfield Library, Thursdays 2 to 4 pm) are a particular source of stimulation and have given rise to five of the poems included in this collection.

Finally, a word of thanks to the devotees of the *open mic* nights at which many of these poems have been read, including at 'Poems and Pints', Button Warehouse, Macclesfield; 'Write and Release', New Mills; 'Petersgate Tap', Stockport; and so on. Much is owed, as you have – perhaps unintentionally – encouraged this author by your enthusiastic response to these readings.

About the Poet

Coming from Nottinghamshire mining stock, Phil Poyser's migration from Mansfield to Macclesfield may seem little more than a minor orthographical change, but it covers a period of over half a century.

Secondary education at the Brunts Grammar School in the late 50s & early 60s was followed by B.Sc. and Ph. D. degrees at Imperial College, London, separated by a gap year travelling overland to Australia (and back) with fellow college dropout, Derek Price.

Post-doctoral research in Concepción, Chile and Strasbourg, France was a prelude to a career as a medicinal chemist in the pharmaceutical industry, firstly in Reims, France and latterly at Alderley Park, Cheshire as ICI Pharmaceuticals evolved into Zeneca Pharmaceuticals and AstraZeneca.

Retirement, or more accurately redundancy, in July, 2007 at last provided the opportunity for Phil to expand his lifelong interest in poetry and led to the publication of two small collections: 'Eric Bloodaxe? And Other Verse' (2014) and 'Seconds Out' (2016). These were well-received, with proceeds going to Prostate Cancer UK.

Poetry continues to be Phil's driving passion and – although delayed by COVID-19 lockdowns and other excursions into the care of the NHS – new selections of works generated by Phil's poetry habit are now available in two further collections, 'Lifelines' and 'BLAA, BLAA, Black Sheep' (both released Autumn 2022).

Along with writing and performing his poems, Phil's personal ABC (allotment, bridge and cycling) complete a packed weekly programme.

In terms of prior publication of these pieces –

'Childhood Photograph' first appeared in 'Poems and Pieces about Childhood', Macclesfield Library Writers and Bollington Bridgend Writers, July, 2012 (proceeds to the NSPCC).

You can find more of Phil's poetry online on his blog:

doggerelbanksy.wordpress.com

Praise for 'Lifelines'

Phil Poyser has a unique way of looking at the world, pulling deft rhymes from the air like rabbits out of hat. In this collection he had taken inspiration from many and varied sources resulting in poems as diverse in theme as his whimsical 'The 'Little Bang' Theory' and 'The Blackberry Jam Scandal'.

In his series of sequences, he includes glimpses of suburban life with glorious bursts of nostalgia as well as presenting us with a chorus line of sonnets that has his words dancing adeptly across the page.

~ Joy Winkler, author of the novel 'Morgan', the plays 'Town' and 'Lightning Under Their Skirts' and collections of her poetry, *inter alia,* 'Stolen Rowan Berries'.

Lifelines is Phil Poyser at his best.
A collection to dip into, connect with, and one you'll
want to read again and again.

> ~ Margaret Holbrook, author ('Cul De Sac
> Tales', 'Picking The Bones' and 'About Us…'),
> playwright and poet ('Hobby Horses Will
> Dance' and 'Not Exactly Life').